hagar

Victoria— Dream big, God does!

𝓔 P~

Rom 11:34-36

hagar

Target of a Jealous Beauty Queen

SHANNON PRIMICERIO

TrueLife Bible Studies

THiNK
P.O. Box 35001
Colorado Springs, Colorado 80935

THiNK is an imprint of NavPress.
THiNK and the THiNK logo are registered trademarks of NavPress. Absence of ® in connection with marks of NavPress or other parties does not indicate an absence of registration of those marks.

ISBN-13: 978-1-60006-113-4
ISBN-10: 1-60006-113-3

Cover design by Charles Brock, The DesignWorks Group, Inc, www.thedesignworksgroup.com
Creative Team: Nicci Hubert, Karen Lee-Thorp, Cara Iverson, Darla Hightower, Arvid Wallen,
    Kathy Guist

Published in association with the Books & Such Literary Agency, Janet Kobobel Grant, 52 Mission Circle, Suite 122, PMB 170, Santa Rosa, CA, 95409-5370, www.booksandsuch.biz.

Printed in the United States of America

1 2 3 4 5 6 / 11 10 09 08 07

FOR A FREE CATALOG OF NAVPRESS BOOKS & BIBLE STUDIES, CALL
1-800-366-7788 (USA) OR 1-800-839-4769 (CANADA).

To Krystal Perrin:

Thanks for the past twenty years of friendship!
I'm looking forward to many more. . .

CONTENTS

THE SUPPORTING ROLE

IF HAGAR'S STORY WERE A movie, she wouldn't be the star. Instead she would play a supporting role to Sarah, Abraham's wife. Hagar's story has always intrigued me because it embodies so many things that I have felt at one time or another: used by others, jealous, insecure, fearful, defiant, and even far from God. Generations and cultural barriers may distance us from Hagar, but the more I read her story, the more certain I am that there are glimpses of Hagar everywhere around us — from the girl next door to the girl in the mirror. I knew a few Hagars in high school, and I have played Hagar in my own life more than once. Of course, her name was never used. But her tendencies came through loud and clear.

I often wish God had told us more about this slave girl who was the victim of manipulation, abuse, and rejection. But her tragedies aren't what I wish I knew more of. No. I wish we were told more about Hagar's strengths. How did she endure time alone with Abraham in his tent when she knew he was just looking for an heir? When she was sent back to face Sarah after enduring a cruel tongue-lashing and who knows what else, how did she muster the grace to let that woman mother the child Hagar herself bore until Sarah had her own son fourteen years later?

Sarah has always been painted as the beautiful matriarch of the children of Israel. She is commended for her faith in regard to the birth of her son Isaac. But to tell you the truth, I'm not all that impressed with her. When you look at her through the lenses of Hagar's story, you see a different picture, and it's not a very flattering one. But Hagar wasn't innocent either. Her relationship with Sarah was a tumultuous wrestling match for power. Theirs is a story of jealousy and betrayal that makes most mean girls look nice.

We are going to spend the bulk of our time together focusing on Hagar's life, but it would be impossible to do so without casting Sarah in a supporting role. I'm sure that in real life it was almost always the other way around.

Perhaps you feel like a supporting character in someone else's story. Maybe you are tired of playing backup to a superstar and you have felt cheated, used, or rejected. Or, in a more honest evaluation, perhaps you have felt downright jealous of the girl who is hogging your spotlight. I've been there before, and so has Hagar. That's what makes her story relevant. It's what makes it worth reading. Let's see what the girl in the supporting role can teach us when she is finally given the spotlight. Hopefully learning from her mistakes will make us more prepared for our spotlights when they come.

HOW TO GET THE MOST OUT OF THIS BIBLE STUDY

YOU HAVE A BUSY LIFE. Homework, sports, and other extra-curricular activities demand a lot of your time. I know that. To make this study easy to fit into your schedule, I have divided Hagar's story into six weeklong segments. But I have not broken each week into daily assignments. It's up to you to find the easiest way for you to get through the material allotted for each week.

In order for you to get the most out of this study, it is vital that you take time to read the assigned passages. The main text for each week is provided for you, but you will be responsible for looking up additional passages on your own. It is also essential that you answer each question thoughtfully and thoroughly. The quizzes and various activities are fun, but they are also important. So don't skip over these portions, thinking you won't get anything out of them.

The ideal way to go through this Bible study is in a small group with some other girls so you can talk through Hagar's story and the questions and issues that come up while exploring it. If you choose to do so, I recommend that you complete the assignments on your own each week and then get together to discuss what you have learned.

This Bible study can also be a tool to help you develop a regular quiet time with God each morning or evening. It's a great way to get into God's Word on a daily basis and study a girl whose life is completely relevant to your own. I suggest you set aside a specific time each day (like six thirty every morning, or eight o'clock every night) and commit to doing a portion of this study. That way, you will stay on track to finish studying Hagar's story in six short weeks.

It is my prayer that through your study of Hagar, you'll come to see and understand that God's Word is real and relevant to your life today.

Grace and peace,

Shannon Primicerio

week one

USED!

> Sarai, Abram's wife, hadn't yet produced a child. She had an Egyptian maid named Hagar. Sarai said to Abram, "GOD has not seen fit to let me have a child. Sleep with my maid. Maybe I can get a family from her." Abram agreed to do what Sarai said.
>
> — GENESIS 16:1-2

INTRODUCTIONS AND FIRST IMPRESSIONS ARE everything. When we meet someone for the first time, we tend to form opinions about the person within the first several minutes. *She's annoying* or *He's cute*, we think to ourselves. And just as we instantly form opinions of others, we know they will quickly shape opinions about us too. So we go to great lengths to ensure that their opinions of us are nothing but complimentary. More often than not, all first impressions are carried into the second meeting. Some first impressions follow people around for the rest of their lives.

FIRST THINGS FIRST

1. Think back to a time when you first met someone you now know well (maybe the first day of school or church camp). What was your first impression of that person?

2. After you got to know that person, how accurate was your first impression?

3. Think about someone you know only casually who made quite an impression on you during your first meeting. Do you still identify that person by something that occurred during your first meeting? (For example, she's the girl who spilled soda on her skirt, or he's the cute guy on the baseball team.) If so, why do you think that is?

4. What do you try to convey about yourself in a first impression?

In Genesis 16:1, we are introduced to Hagar this way: "[Sarai] had an Egyptian maid named Hagar." Amazing how one small sentence can say so much.

5. List at least three things you learn about Hagar from this introduction.

6. What images does the word slave conjure up in your mind?

7. Read Genesis 12:11. What impression do you get of Sarai?

8. How do you think Hagar felt in comparison to Sarai?

9. What leads you to believe that?

10. How do you think Sarai thought of Hagar?

11. What makes you think that?

12. Have you ever felt like a Hagar in comparison to a Sarai? Explain.

Back in Genesis 12, before we are ever introduced to Hagar by name, we are given insights into life in Egypt and possibly discover how Hagar came to be Sarai's maid. Read the following passage, Genesis 12:10-20, before proceeding:

Then a famine came to the land. Abram went down to Egypt to live; it was a hard famine. As he drew near to Egypt, he said to his wife, Sarai, "Look. We both know that you're a beautiful woman. When the Egyptians see you they're going to say, 'Aha! That's his wife!' and kill me. But they'll let you live. Do me a favor: tell them you're my sister. Because of you, they'll welcome me and let me live."

When Abram arrived in Egypt, the Egyptians took one look and saw that his wife was stunningly beautiful. Pharaoh's princes raved over her to Pharaoh. She was taken to live with Pharaoh.

Because of her, Abram got along very well: he accumulated sheep and cattle, male and female donkeys, *men and women servants*, and camels. But GOD hit Pharaoh hard because of Abram's wife Sarai; everybody in the palace got seriously sick.

Pharaoh called for Abram, "What's this that you've done to me? Why didn't you tell me that she's your wife? Why did you say, 'She's my sister' so that I'd take her as my wife?

Here's your wife back — take her and get out!"

Pharaoh ordered his men to get Abram out of the country. They sent him and his wife and everything he owned on their way. (Emphasis added)

In a time of famine, Egypt was the land of plenty. People, Abram and Sarai included, went to Egypt to escape want. Although Hagar more than likely came from a family of slaves, she was still surrounded by the finest luxuries. It is believed that prior to Abram and Sarai's visit to Egypt, Hagar was in service somewhere in Pharaoh's palace. Many scholars believe that she was one of the gifts Pharaoh gave Abram in verse 16.[1] Simply put, Hagar was a gift given to Abram and Sarai because Sarai was very beautiful. I don't know about you, but that sure wouldn't make me like Sarai. As if being a slave weren't bad enough, Hagar had to be the slave of a beautiful woman — who *knew* she was beautiful.

I remember some of the girls who were known as the "pretty and popular" ones when I was in junior high and high school. They weren't always the most pleasant to be around. Usually they talked down to others, behaved rudely, and used other people for their own gain. When I was in college, however, I met a girl who had been treated very badly by some of the pretty and popular types when she was in high school. We'll call her Stephanie. She was the type of girl who blossomed overnight, and although her high school days were filled with awkwardness and heartache, she was a real knockout by the time she arrived at college.

When I met Stephanie, I was taken aback by how kind and considerate she was of others. She was always helping a new student find his or her way around campus, and she constantly smiled and said hello to anyone she walked by. She is the type of beautiful that I prefer to be around. But something tells me that Sarai didn't exactly fit into this mold. To top it all off, her name means "princess" to Hagar's "immigrant" or "fugitive."[2] Somehow I'm getting the impression that Sarai thought her name fit her very well.

Let's read about some of Sarai's interactions with Hagar in Genesis 16:1-3:

> Sarai, Abram's wife, hadn't yet produced a child. She had an Egyptian maid named Hagar. Sarai said to Abram, "GOD has not seen fit to let me have a child. Sleep with my maid. Maybe I can get a family from her." Abram agreed to do what Sarai said.
>
> So Sarai, Abram's wife, took her Egyptian maid Hagar and gave her to her husband Abram as a wife. Abram had been living ten years in Canaan when this took place.

We've already established that Hagar was introduced to us as Sarai's slave. But in the very same sentence that we see her as a slave, we also see her as something else: a solution. And not just any solution — she was *the* solution to Sarai's problems (or so Sarai thought). Suddenly this slave girl with little value became of extreme importance to Sarai. And Sarai used Hagar to get what she wanted: a son. Without producing an heir (son) for Abram, Sarai was viewed as a worthless wife back in her day. So it was of great significance to her to find a way to have a son, even if it were through the use of a surrogate mother. Not wanting to feel worthless herself, the "princess" used Hagar for her own gain.

13. If you were Hagar, how would you feel about marrying your mistress's husband so that you could produce a child for the two of them?

14. In this situation, do you think Sarai had any regard for Hagar and her feelings? Explain your answer.

15. Describe a modern-day situation in which one girl could use another girl for her own gain.

16. If you have ever been in a situation like the one you described, were you in Sarai's position or Hagar's? Describe how you felt and why you made the choices you did.

17. Why do you think it is sometimes so easy to disregard the feelings of someone else when what we want is at stake?

WORDS TO LIVE BY

In Philippians 2:1-4, the apostle Paul offers some instructions regarding this mentality that are worth memorizing. So grab a pen and a 3x5 card and jot down these verses. Spend this week working on memorizing them.

> If you've gotten anything at all out of following Christ, if his love has made any difference in your life, if being in a community of the Spirit means anything to you, if you have a heart, if you *care* — then do me a favor: Agree with each other, love each other, be deep-spirited friends. Don't push your way to the front; don't sweet-talk your way to the top. Put yourself aside, and help others get ahead. Don't be obsessed with getting your own advantage. Forget yourselves long enough to lend a helping hand.

18. What are some things you sometimes do to "push your way to the front" or "sweet-talk your way to the top"?

19. How can you turn those things around this week and begin to "put yourself aside, and help others get ahead" instead?

AN IMPORTANT TOPIC TO MENTION

I know that not everyone who participates in this Bible study will deal firsthand with the topic I am about to address. But I also know there will be more than a few girls who will. And it is important information for all of us to pay attention to so we can better protect ourselves and help others through difficult situations.

Girls have enough problems being used by other girls who want to manipulate others for their own gain. But there is one problem that may bear even greater consequences down the line, and that is when a girl becomes physically used by a guy. It has been said that "guys will give love for sex, and girls will give sex for love." In all of my years of ministry, I have, unfortunately, found that statement to be true.

I'm almost certain that I am writing to four categories of girls right now: those who have never been physically intimate with a guy in any way and wouldn't dream of it before marriage, those who have had some sort of physical involvement with a guy and now regret it, those who are currently in a relationship in which they are being too intimate with a guy, and those who are toying with the idea of taking a relationship to the next level in physical intimacy. Please note that

I do not exclusively mean sex when I say physical involvement. There are kisses and other touches that can be extremely intimate. In fact, there are prayers and spiritual conversations that can be shared that are far more intimate than any physical contact. So it's a good idea for those of you who aren't physical with a guy to pay attention too.

As girls, it is in our very nature to nurture those we love. We're affectionate creatures at the core. For example, when a group of your friends arrives at a gathering, I am sure that all of the girls usually run up and hug each other, whereas the guys might hang back from the crowd a little and look around awkwardly (unless they are hugging the girls). For some reason, most guys get weirded out when it comes to hugging other guys. But girls don't have that problem. So it is only natural for us, when we get into a relationship with a guy we care deeply about, to want to express our affection for him on a level that is different from the affection we express to our friends. *If I hug my friends and they're just my friends, I need to do something else with this guy to show him I feel differently about him,* we rationalize. But that mentality almost always has costly consequences.

Anytime you give a piece of your heart or your body to a guy you are not married to, you are giving away something you will never get back to a guy who hasn't promised that he will stay (and a promise isn't a promise until there is a ring on your finger and you have said your vows). In most cases, relationships that turn physical before the wedding day never make it to a wedding day. And those that do create problems in intimacy that a couple will have to work through at a later time.

For most of us, intimacy doesn't stop in the physical realm. Most of us tend to be talkers too. And because we are talkers, we love to divulge all kinds of personal information about ourselves — dreams, goals, aspirations — to anyone willing to listen. So sometimes we openly share our hearts with a guy we are interested in, and before we know it he gets freaked out and runs off, leaving us feeling betrayed and defiled. I know this because I was once one of the girls I just described. In my four years of high school, I had only one serious crush. We were friends, and we talked a lot — on the phone, in person, sometimes even paired off when a big group of our friends was hanging out. And then one day he was gone. Without any warning, he fell for another girl and left me nursing a broken heart and wishing I hadn't told him so much about my dreams. It took a long time for me to get over the pain. In the end of that friendship, I felt very used. Looking back I can see that I was just the girl this guy hung out with until someone better came along. For years I felt as if I was the only one who had experienced this.

Then I became an author and the e-mails started piling in. They ranged from the physical, "I lost my virginity at fourteen and now I feel worthless and used up," to the spiritual, "My boyfriend and I prayed and did devotions together every day, and then out of the blue he broke up with me and now I feel so lost," to the confused, "I have this boyfriend, but he's not really my boyfriend although he acts like he is." When about the twentieth e-mail came, I realized I was far from alone.

In my book *Being a Girl Who Leads*, I devote one entire chapter to guarding your heart emotionally and spiritually in friendships and other relationships with guys, and another chapter to protecting your purity in those same relationships. If this section has somehow struck a nerve with you, I suggest you pick up a copy of that book for further study.

Feeling used is never fun, but it is never more devastating than when you feel as if you have given a part of yourself to someone who didn't care enough to stick around. For those of you who haven't yet been in that situation, please, please be careful. Do not share parts of yourself that you want to preserve (and that God wants you to preserve) for marriage. And for those of you who feel as if it is already too late for you, please know that God delights in restoring those of us who have made mistakes, and He delights in working through us again. Throughout Hagar's story, we will see that both Sarai and Hagar became women who played great roles in the plans of a God who loved them both dearly. That can be your future too if you will choose to make some changes.

Talk with a youth leader or trusted adult and confess the

baggage you are carrying. Pray with that leader and ask God for forgiveness. Then correct the areas that need changing. You are not alone in all of this.

If your issue goes much deeper than that and you have been a victim of rape or sexual abuse, please ask a trusted adult to get you connected with professional counseling. You do not need to be ashamed of what has happened to you. Please go and seek wholeness and restoration for yourself.

Because we are all at different places in this area, the next few questions are going to be more open-ended than most. Please answer them as they pertain to you.

20. What are some ways in which you never want to feel used?

21. How can you prevent those things from happening?

22. What are some areas in your life where you realize you need to make a conscious effort to protect yourself from being used by a boy? (For example, in conversations with a guy you have a crush on, or in physical boundaries with your boyfriend.) Be specific about how you need to protect yourself.

23. If you feel that you've been used by someone, it is important to get help so you can heal from all you have been through. Name one safe adult in your life whom you can talk to.

Setting standards is important in your relationships with the opposite sex. You can't wait until you are in a situation to figure out how you are going to handle it. If you do, your emotions might lead you astray. When my husband and I were dating, we decided we would never be alone together. For us this meant we would be in a car together only if we were on a public street driving to a public destination. This way, we weren't alone since people we knew could drive by and look in the windows at any minute. If we went out to dinner, just the two of us, we weren't really alone because we were surrounded by other people. If we were at my house, my parents were home and awake, and we were in the living room knowing they could walk in on us at any minute. Knowing that people could always see what we were doing kept us accountable in ways we desperately needed. Our definition of *not alone* might seem broad to some, but it worked for us. We were able to build a relationship outside the atmosphere of a group (which is important in a relationship moving toward marriage), but we also had a safe environment that kept us out of trouble. It is important to note that my husband and I were both in our early twenties when we started dating, so these standards aren't reserved for when you are in high school.

24. Write out a list of standards that will be your own personal Code of Conduct for relationships with the opposite sex. Once you have completed it, copy it onto another sheet of paper and give it to a friend who can hold you accountable. Because I think it is important, I filled in the first answer on your list for you.

   a. I will never be alone (outside of a public place) with a guy who is not a family member. (This will save you more trouble than you can even imagine.)

   b.

   c.

   d.

   e.

Talking It Out

The God who loved us so much that He sent His only Son to die for us will never use or abandon us the way some people will. If Hagar's story offers us any hope, it is this: God is willing to chase us down and wrap us in His love when we feel used and begin running scared. Write out a prayer right now thanking God for His fervent love for you.

Writing It Down

Jot down a few things that really stood out to you in this week's lesson. Make sure to note why those things stuck out to you.

Setting a Higher Standard

List one new goal you have for yourself as a result of this week's lesson. Make it a specific goal and then break it down into smaller, easier-to-read steps. (For instance, "My goal is to protect myself from being used by guys in the future. I will start by setting some standards for those relationships.") Put today's date next to your goal so you can come back and check your progress in a few months.

week two

LESSONS LEARNED FROM SARAI

So Sarai, Abram's wife, took her
Egyptian maid Hagar and gave her to
her husband Abram as a wife. . . . He
slept with Hagar and she got pregnant.

— GENESIS 16:3-4

NOTHING IS WORSE THAN BEING around someone who has what you want and knows it. In high school I had a friend who had a crush on the same guy I did. Eventually he stopped spending so much time with me and began going out with her. One night she called and flat-out asked me if I had feelings for him. I lied and told her I didn't, because I didn't trust her with the truth.

"Good," she practically spat into the phone. "I didn't want this to be a *silent* competition." That phone call ended our friendship. Her attitude about the fact that this guy had chosen her over me was so ugly that she was hard to be around. People probably thought I was too heartbroken to hang out with this girl and her new boyfriend, but the honest truth was she was so condescending toward me about the whole thing that my heartache seemed miniscule in comparison to her ego. No one wants to be around a world-class flaunter. It's just not fun.

In Hagar's story we will see that she and Sarai take turns flaunting their victories in each other's faces, and it isn't pretty. This week starts the competition off when Hagar conceives a child after sleeping with Abram. Read Genesis 16:3-4 to gain the proper context for this week's study:

> So Sarai, Abram's wife, took her Egyptian maid Hagar and gave her to her husband Abram as a wife. Abram had been living ten years in Canaan when this took place. He slept with Hagar and she got pregnant. When she learned she was pregnant, she looked down on her mistress.

This was a situation in which both women were clearly wrong. Sarai didn't heed God's command that marriage should be between one man and one woman. Instead she gave in to the cultural trends of her times and gave her maid to her husband as a second wife so that she could get heirs. When she got exactly what she wanted, she wasn't happy. (Side note: In Sarai's day, using your maid to get heirs was a form of surrogate motherhood. When the baby was born, he or she was taken directly from the birth mother and placed in the lap of the mistress to signify adoption. Usually the birth mother had no motherly rights.) It's also important to note that Sarai and Hagar didn't receive equal status as Abram's wives. Sarai was still his wife, while Hagar was viewed as more of a concubine and was still viewed as Sarai's slave.

CULTURALLY RELEVANT

1. Make a list of five things our culture says are acceptable even though God says they are wrong. I will fill in the first answer for you.

   a. Having sex outside of marriage.

   b.

c.

d.

e.

2. Sarai could have rationalized her decision by claiming it was the only way Abram would have heirs. Pick one of your answers from question 1 and list several rationalizations people offer for why they think it is okay.

3. Is it dangerous to make a judgment based on whether or not something is culturally acceptable? Why or why not?

4. What role does culture (specifically pop culture) play in some of the decisions you make? Answer specifically for the following categories:

   a. Clothing:

b. Movies/Television:

c. Music:

d. Language:

e. Attitude toward your parents:

"IT'S NOT A BIG DEAL"

When I was in college, my friends and I all used to cram into one dorm room on Thursday nights and end our week by watching a popular sitcom together. A few weeks into our new ritual, my friend "Christina" shared that she was convicted by the show because the lifestyles of some of the characters were contrary to how we should behave as Christians. We all shrugged her off and told her it was no big deal. Several seasons later, the underlying raunchiness of the show got to the rest of us and we gave up on watching it. But by then it was too late.

Christina began making poor lifestyle choices and even imitated some of the behaviors she had witnessed on this show. When another friend of mine confronted her on it, she claimed, "You watched the characters on that show do these things for years and you didn't have a problem with it. So don't even begin to tell me why these things are wrong for me." We were all stunned. Her rationale didn't make her behavior right, but it did show the rest of us that we were very wrong when we told her that watching a show like that wasn't a big deal.

I don't want you to think that I am saying everything associated with pop culture is bad. In fact, it can be the total opposite if we learn to be discerning about what we say, watch, wear, or listen to. Some of the most effective conversations I have had with non-Christians come when I am sitting in my hairdresser's chair being cut and colored according to the latest style.

As Christians, we can become effective tools for God's kingdom if we can successfully show the world that Jesus Christ came not to make nerds of all mankind but to redeem mankind from its sins. We don't need to hide ourselves in a Christian bubble, either. Exposing ourselves to a culture that is entirely Christian may protect us, but it won't do the world any good. We are called to make disciples, and we can't do that if we hide from anything "non-Christian."

USING CULTURE FOR GOD'S GLORY

5. What are some ways you can use popular things in our culture to witness to non-Christians?

6. Think of the last movie you saw (Christian movies don't count). What was the movie? What themes did it have that could be used to point others to their need for Christ?

My answer: *Cinderella Man* with Russell Crowe. This movie is a true story based on legendary boxer James J. Braddock and his tumultuous career as a professional boxer in the Depression era. Braddock lost everything he had — career, fame, and fortune — but fought to keep what was really important, his family. It's a movie about knowing what you are fighting for, and it invokes passion in the hearts of those who view it. Non-Christians could benefit from asking themselves what they're fighting for, because many would come to realize that their lives are empty and meaningless without Christ.

IT'S NOT JUST ABOUT CULTURE

This week's lesson isn't just about culture. It's also about Sarai's need to control her circumstances and Hagar's attitude when she was finally given something of value.

We learned last week that Sarai was outwardly beautiful. Not only did she have the attention of her husband but she succeeded in turning other heads as well (remember Pharaoh?). Beauty in and of itself is not a bad thing. I'll be the first person to admit that I spend several hours parked in front of a mirror doing my best to make myself beautiful before I leave my house. But beauty can quickly become a bad thing if we let ourselves think that our beauty somehow makes us superior to others or deserving of great things.

When I read about Sarai in Scripture, I get the impression that she didn't lack for much. People who don't lack for much can easily become accustomed to thinking they are in control of their environments. So, not surprisingly, God gave Sarai a part of her life that she couldn't control: her inability to bear children.

7. Why do you think God chose childbearing as the area in which Sarai had no control? (Hint: Think about her culture and the things they valued.)

8. How did she respond to her lack of control in this area?

9. Would you describe yourself as someone who likes to be in control? Why or why not?

10. How do you tend to behave in situations where you are not in control of your circumstances or environment?

Read Genesis 21:1-7:

GOD visited Sarah exactly as he said he would; GOD did to Sarah what he promised: Sarah became pregnant and gave Abraham a son in his old age, and at the very time God had set. Abraham named him Isaac. When his son was eight days old, Abraham circumcised him just as God had commanded.

Abraham was a hundred years old when his son Isaac was born.

Sarah said,

> God has blessed me with laughter
> and all who get the news will laugh with me!

She also said,

> Whoever would have suggested to Abraham
> that Sarah would one day nurse a baby!
> Yet here I am! I've given the old man a son!

11. When did Sarah give Abraham a son? Fill in the blanks below:

_____ became pregnant and gave Abraham a ____

in his old age, and at _____

_____.

Often we wrestle with God about things that are beyond our control. But what we fail to realize is that in many cases, God isn't withholding the thing we want forever but just until the timing is right. About fourteen years passed between the birth of Hagar's son and the birth of Sarah's, and in those years God had many things to teach both women. I am almost positive that one thing God taught Sarah in that time was that she needed to let go of her need to control.

12. Is there an area in your life that you need to surrender control of? If so, what is it?

13. What can help you let go of your desire to control?

SIMPLE MISJUDGMENTS CAN EQUAL MAJOR TROUBLE

I don't know about you, but I like to be in control. For some reason I just feel safer that way. But really we are safe only when we are inside God's will for our lives. Sometimes our wills clash strongly against God's and sin enters the picture. Our judgment isn't always as good as we think it is. I have a family member who has an alcohol problem, and he recently thought it would be okay to get behind the wheel of a car after he had been drinking. Thankfully he didn't kill anyone, but he did get arrested. He has spent time in jail and is now in rehab as a result. Sometimes other factors can impair our judgment the way alcohol impaired the thinking of my loved one.

14. Make a list of five things that can impair a person's judgment when making decisions. I have filled in the first blank for you.

    a. Greed

    b.

    c.

    d.

    e.

What we fail to realize most of the time is that those of us who like to be in control the most are the least able to actually remain controlled when things don't go our way. Let's look at Genesis 16:5-7 to see how Sarai responded once Hagar became pregnant and flaunted it in front of her:

> Sarai told Abram, "It's all your fault that I'm suffering this abuse. I put my maid in bed with you and the minute she knows she's pregnant, she treats me like I'm nothing. May GOD decide which of us is right."

"You decide," said Abram. "Your maid is your business."

Sarai was abusive to Hagar and Hagar ran away.

15. How did Sarai treat Abram when things didn't go her way?

16. How did she treat Hagar?

I don't know about you, but I have had my fair share of moments when I responded as Sarai did. Blaming others and acting out in anger are two natural responses to not being in control. But that doesn't make them right.

17. How do you typically react when things are out of your control? (Examples: "I blame other people." "I act out in anger." "I blame myself and obsess on my flaws." "I get depressed and eat ice cream.")

18. Why do you think that is?

It is important to remember that neither of the options Sarai chose will yield us the results we desire. Sarai's anger and blame shifting didn't cause her to get pregnant and have her own son, and it also didn't get rid of the fact that Hagar had a son. As people with limited knowledge and perspective, we were not designed with the ability to control our own lives. God has given us the ability to make choices, but He hasn't equipped us to run the whole show.

WORDS TO LIVE BY

Pull out another 3x5 card and jot down this week's memory verse. Remember to put it somewhere you will see it often, and repeat it aloud to yourself several times so it will stick with you.

We can make our plans,
    but the LORD determines our steps. (Proverbs 16:9, NLT)

The Lord is ultimately the One who is in control. If we can learn to recognize this sooner, we might be able to prevent ourselves from becoming so out of control when things don't go according to our own plans.

ARE YOU A CONTROL FREAK?

Take the following quiz to gauge how much you like to be in control. Circle the answer that best corresponds with how you would behave.

A = Always, S = Sometimes, N = Never

1. All week long you make plans to have some friends sleep over
    for the weekend. An hour before they are supposed to arrive,
    one friend calls and says she forgot about a family event and
    has to cancel. Another friend is offered a babysitting job
    and really needs the money, so she can't make it either. You
    respond in an irritated tone and plan to remind them that you
    are unhappy with them every day of next week. After all, real
    friends would never do this to you.

    A   S   N

2. You have been looking forward to the school dance for
    months. But the morning of the dance, your grandma calls to
    say that your grandpa broke his leg and is in the hospital. Your
    mom tells you that you can't go to the dance because you have
    to go with your family to stay with your grandma. You respond
    by yelling at your mom and running into your room. You slam
    the door, shouting, "It's not fair!"

    A   S   N

3. The guy you have been crushin' on is having a birthday party
    — and you're invited! You go out and buy a new top just for
    the occasion. Thirty minutes before you are supposed to leave,
    as you are finishing your makeup, your little sister comes in
    your room with your new shirt in her hand. "I borrowed this
    last night," she says, "and I spilled soda on it. I'm sorry." You
    respond by screaming at her and yanking your shirt out of her
    hands as you run down the hallway to get her in serious trou-
    ble. Doesn't she know she ruined your night?

    A   S   N

4. Your best friend's parents agree to let you guys go see your
    favorite band in concert on a school night, as long as your
    friend finishes her homework. Since you planned in advance,

yours is done early. Thirty minutes before you were to meet your friend, she calls and tells you she can't go anymore. Your parents won't let you go without her. You respond by yelling at your friend, and when she bursts into tears, you ask to talk to her parents to see if you can persuade them to let her go.

A   S   N

5. Your dad loses his job just before your new soccer season starts. Dejectedly he tells you he's sorry he can't buy you new cleats and you will have to use your old ones. When you get to your first practice and see that you are the only girl without new cleats, you tell everyone else on your team that you have to wear last year's cleats because you have mean parents.

A   S   N

6. For the last six weeks, you have been walking on cloud nine because you are going out with the cutest boy in school. The day before Valentine's Day, he dumps you — breaking your heart and ruining your plans. You spend all of Valentine's Day telling your friends how stupid he is and giving him the evil eye.

A   S   N

7. When your teacher posts test scores, you notice that you got the lowest grade in your class. Later that day, you approach her to explain why your grade was so low. "My dad went on a business trip and my book was in the back of his car, so I couldn't study," you say sweetly as you try to get her to change your grade. When that doesn't work, you tell everyone how much you hate that teacher.

A   S   N

8. It's your senior year and your parents have decided you are old enough to date. But they also decide that your younger sister, who is a sophomore, can date too. You respond by arguing

with your parents about how unfair that is, and you refuse to let your sister borrow a sweater for her first date.

A   S   N

9. For weeks you have been dropping hints about the new iPod you want for your birthday. When your parents surprise you with a new CD player instead, you burst into tears and spend the rest of the day moping around.

   A   S   N

10. To celebrate your high school graduation, all of your friends are going on a road trip, but your parents won't let you go. You lock yourself in your room and refuse to talk to them for a week.

    A   S   N

Now let's see what your answers mean.

Mostly A's = Anger Management. You need to learn how to reel it in, Girlfriend. Control might as well be your middle name. I would venture to guess that Sarai's story is ringing true for you, since you have found yourself shifting blame and acting out in anger on more than one occasion. Memorize Proverbs 16:9 and stop trying to control absolutely everything. Sit back and let God do His job. Your circumstances will turn out much better if you do.

Mostly S's = Work in Progress. It seems as if you are learning to work though your tendency to try to control other people and your circumstances. But you aren't all the way there yet. Commit Proverbs 16:9 to memory and take a deep breath before reacting to something that is out of your control.

Mostly N's = Mellow Yellow. You are more of a go-with-the-flow type, and being in control doesn't seem to be your thing. Or maybe you're a timid personality who wishes she had more control but feel you have none, so why bother? Maybe you identify with Hagar the slave, who knew she had to do what other people said. Commit

Proverbs 16:9 to memory and continue to relinquish control of your life to God. Also, take necessary precautions to make sure you aren't simply surrendering control to others.

Hopefully this little exercise helped you realize just how much you like to control things. Becoming aware of a problem is the first step in conquering it. As we will see through the lives of Hagar and Sarai, sometimes we have to learn the same lesson more than once before we see results.

Talking It Out

Write out a prayer to God asking Him to help you become strong against the pressures of pop culture and help you submit to His authority when things are out of your control. He loves you and desires the best for you.

Writing It Down

Look back through this week's lesson and find the point that resonated the most with you. Take a few moments and reflect on how that point applies to your daily life. Discern what areas you may need to change.

Setting a Higher Standard

Create one new goal for yourself as a result of this week's lesson. Make sure to break it down into smaller, easier-to-reach steps. And put a date next to it so you can come back and check your progress.

week three

HAGAR'S HAUGHTY ATTITUDE

When [Hagar] learned she was pregnant,
she looked down on her mistress.

—GENESIS 16:4

LAST WEEK WE LOOKED AT some of the mistakes Sarai made in her relationship with Hagar. This week we are going to focus on some of the mistakes Hagar made in her relationship with Sarai. Girls are catty. Many of the girls I knew growing up were mean. I'm sure some of them thought I was mean too. In junior high I even got called into the principal's office to settle a dispute over a yelling match I got into with a girl who had made fun of my family. Those weren't good times, and they aren't years I remember too fondly.

I don't know why it is exactly, but sometimes we use someone else's misbehavior as an excuse for our own sin. "Well, they started it," we rationalize. But to God that is never an acceptable answer. It doesn't matter how Sarai treated Hagar. There was no excuse for the haughty attitude Hagar adopted toward her mistress.

1. Think of a conflict you have had with a friend, sibling, or class-mate. Looking back, can you see how both parties played a part in the situation? Explain what happened.

Please read this week's primary passage:

So Sarai, Abram's wife, took her Egyptian maid Hagar and gave her to her husband Abram as a wife. Abram had been living ten years in Canaan when this took place. He slept with Hagar and she got pregnant. When she learned she was pregnant, she looked down on her mistress. (Genesis 16:3-4)

The Bible tells us that Hagar "looked down on her mistress," or in other translations "despised" her. It seems to me that Hagar developed an unhealthy pride once she became pregnant.

2. How would you define looking down on someone else?

3. Have you ever been looked down upon? If so, how did it make you feel?

Think about Hagar's life as a slave. Having nothing, she spent most of her life being looked down upon by other people. But suddenly, when she became pregnant and provided an heir for Abram, the tables turned. Sometimes drastic changes in circumstances are accompanied by drastic changes in demeanor. Even if Hagar didn't like Sarai before this happened, I'm sure she didn't look down on her. She didn't have a reason to.

4. How would you explain the sudden change in how Hagar viewed Sarai?

5. Describe a time in your life when you, or someone you know, experienced a change in circumstances that ultimately resulted in a change in demeanor as well. What happened? Was the change for the better or the worse? Explain.

WORDS TO LIVE BY

Write this passage out on a 3x5 card and commit it to memory this week. Stick your card someplace you will see it daily (in your Bible, on your mirror, or in your school binder). Ask a friend to quiz you on your progress so you can make sure you are really committing it to memory. This passage is one we all could benefit from knowing by heart.

> "Do you want to stand out? Then step down. Be a servant. If you puff yourself up, you'll get the wind knocked out of you. But if you're content to simply be yourself, your life will count for plenty." (Matthew 23:11-12)

6. According to this passage, how should we respond to delightful changes in our circumstances?

7. What role, if any, do you think insecurity played in Hagar's puffed-up attitude? Explain your answer.

Arrogance is almost always fueled by insecurity. Even if it seems as though arrogant people think they are the greatest thing ever, more often than not they feel as if they really aren't worth anything at all. They try to make others feel smaller so they will feel bigger.

I am an only child, so growing up I always had the latest and greatest stuff. Since there was only one of me, my parents were able to provide me with luxuries my friends with many siblings never had. Sometimes I bragged about what I got for Christmas or my birthday in an attempt to make people think I was a friend worth having (if they hung out with me they could use my stuff). To some people my bragging sounded like arrogance, when in reality it was insecurity talking as I tried to bribe people into being my friends.

8. Does this change the way you view the arrogant people in your life? Why or why not?

9. Think about your own moments of arrogance or insecurity (come on, we all have them occasionally). How do you see those two things working together in your own behavior?

ARROGANCE VS. INSECURITY

Take the following quiz to see how well you can discern between arrogance and insecurity. Circle "A" for every statement that describes arrogance, "I" for statements describing insecurity, and "B" for statements describing both.

1. Your friend gets a new haircut that slightly resembles yours, so you run to the mirror to check your hair and compare the two styles.

   A   I   B

2. One of your guy friends, whom you have a crush on, tells you he likes the new girl in class. You lie to him and say that you heard she has a long-distance boyfriend she's practically engaged to.

   A   I   B

3. When you get a better grade on the algebra test than your best friend who tutored you, you make sure to flaunt it and tell all of your friends.

   A   I   B

4. When you meet your boyfriend's parents for the first time, you rattle off a list of your accomplishments so they can see how lucky their son is to have someone like you in his life.

   A   I   B

5. Another girl in your class spreads a rumor about you so that no one asks you to the school dance. You respond by loudly telling her how wrong she was in front of a large crowd of people at lunch.

   A   I   B

6. One of your teachers makes a comment about how your older sister was a brighter student than you are, and you instantly defend yourself by stating all of the things you are good at that your sister isn't.

   A   I   B

7. You win the title of Homecoming Queen and instantly think that means you are more popular, and much prettier, than the other four nominees.

   A   I   B

Correct Answers:
Questions 1, 2, 5, and 6: Insecurity. Questions 3, 4, and 7: Both.

Hopefully that quiz showed you that it is possible to be insecure without being arrogant, but it really isn't possible to be arrogant without being insecure in some way. Both arrogance and insecurity are sinful attitudes because they are forms of self-focus. I know that can be hard to believe. But when we are constantly thinking poorly of ourselves, we're still spending a lot of time thinking about ourselves. Thinking negative thoughts about ourselves doesn't somehow make our thoughts more holy. God doesn't want us to be consumed with ourselves in any capacity. Instead, He wants us to focus on Him and what we can do with our individual gifts and personalities to bring others into His kingdom.

10. When you think of arrogance and insecurity both being forms of sin, how does that make you feel? Why?

11. We have mentioned that both behaviors are forms of self-focus, but how are the two behaviors different?

12. Do these differences make it easier to give in to one over the other?

Looking back on Hagar and Sarai's story, we can see that both women suffered from insecurity and paid some high prices for it. Some of Sarai's consequences became evident last week, while Hagar's will continue to unfold over time. I'll be honest with you: Insecurity is something I have battled for years. In junior high school I was so unsure of myself that I was afraid to go to the counter in a fast-food restaurant and ask for extra packets of ketchup. Over time, God has worked on me in this area, but I still struggle. One thing that helps me get over my own insecurities is reaching out and helping others overcome their insecurities.

13. Make a list of three people you know who are either extremely arrogant or extremely insecure.

    a.

    b.

    c.

14. How do you normally respond to their arrogant or insecure attitudes?

15. Pick the most arrogant person you put on your list. Knowing what you learned this week, explain how you see his or her insecurities playing into his or her arrogance.

16. Do these insights make it easier to love this person? Why or why not?

When I was in high school, I decided to call a guy from our youth group who I hadn't seen in quite some time. He had been mean to me on more than one occasion, so we didn't really talk outside of youth group even though I had access to his phone number. I took a shot and called him one night and told him that a couple of us missed seeing him around. He was nice but somewhat standoffish on the phone. When we hung up, I felt a little dumb for calling. A few days later, he told his dad he had been having one of his lowest moments ever when I called. He said that call picked up his spirits for an entire week. Thankfully God let me hear about this. Otherwise I would have spent the next few days feeling like a complete idiot. If the Lord leads you to, go out of your comfort zone on behalf of someone else. Even if it doesn't seem that it means anything to that person, deep down it probably will.

17. Can you think of a time when someone else's kind gesture helped build up your confidence? If so, explain.

Talking It Out

Take some time and write out a prayer asking God to help you in the areas you tend to struggle most. You may want to go back and look over some of your answers before writing out your prayer.

Writing It Down

Now that you have spent some time sharing your thoughts with God, jot down some personal reflections on how you feel about the things you learned this week. Were any of those lessons surprising to you? Why or why not?

Setting a Higher Standard

In light of this week's lesson, think of one new goal you would like to set for yourself. Write it down, and next to it write the first step you are going to take toward accomplishing it. Then sign it and date it so you can look back on when you first decided to make this change in your life.

week four

GOING BACK IN ORDER TO GO FORWARD

The angel of the LORD found Hagar beside a desert spring along the road to Shur. The angel said to her, "Hagar, Sarai's servant, where have you come from, and where are you going?"

—GENESIS 16:7-8 (NLT)

HAVE YOU EVER RUN AWAY from a situation (or person) that hurt you? I know I have. Many of us have never been physically assaulted in our lives, but I'm almost positive that all of us have had to endure verbal abuse of some sort. The old saying, "Sticks and stones may break my bones, but words will never hurt me," is one of the biggest lies we have ever been asked to buy into. Skinned knees and broken bones heal over time, but verbal assaults usually leave gaping wounds that forever alter our personalities and dispositions. For some reason, the hurtful words of other people seem to affect the way we ultimately see ourselves. If someone tells us we are ugly, suddenly we feel ugly. The same is true when someone tells us we are stupid or unpopular.

I went through high school petrified to take a test of any kind because *one* teacher in the eighth grade told me that I was smart but didn't test well. With his one comment, a new chorus was birthed in my mind. *You may know your stuff,* this chorus sang before every test, *but you aren't a good test taker.* More often than not I was defeated long before I ever sat down with a Scantron and a number two pencil.

Last week we caught a glimpse of an insecure yet arrogant version of Hagar. But this week we will see her in quite a different light. We'll learn that Hagar endured such intense abuse from Sarai that she ran wildly from her presence. Through her story we will come to understand what makes us run from others in the first place and how we can find the healing we need in order to face what is in front of us. We will break the text for this week's lesson into three sections. Let's begin by reading our first portion of text:

> Then Sarai said to Abram, "It's all your fault! Now this servant of mine is pregnant, and she despises me, though I myself gave her the privilege of sleeping with you. The LORD will make you pay for doing this to me!"
>
> Abram replied, "Since she is your servant, you may deal with her as you see fit." So Sarai treated her harshly, and Hagar ran away. (Genesis 16:5-6, NLT)

HARSH TREATMENT

1. Knowing what you do about Sarai and Hagar, what sort of harsh treatment do you think Sarai subjected Hagar to?

2. Think back to a time in your life when you were treated harshly. How did this harsh treatment affect you? Has it left a lasting mark on your personality or how you see yourself? Explain.

3. The Bible doesn't tell us that Hagar had anywhere specific to run to, yet she ran away anyway. Why did she run if she had nowhere to go?

4. Describe a time in your life when you ran away from someone or something. Did you have somewhere specific to run to for safety and comfort? What was it that motivated you to run in the first place? (Running is used in a figurative sense in this question. Perhaps you just stopped hanging out with someone who hurt your feelings. That would count as running in this case.)

WORDS TO LIVE BY

Pull out a pen and a 3x5 card and write down this week's memory verse. This is an important one that can easily come in handy in a variety of different circumstances. Ultimately, this is one of those verses that you simply *must* know.

> GOD's name is a place of protection—
>   good people can run there and be safe. (Proverbs 18:10)

Even when we have nowhere else to run, we can always run to the Lord. He's not just there for the big things; He's there for all things. I learned this for the first time when I was thirteen years old. As I sat in my bedroom crying my eyes out over some hurtful things some other girls had said about me at school, I picked up my Bible. It fell open to Psalm 30:5, which says, "The nights of crying your eyes out give way to days of laughter." In that moment, I knew that God cared about the things in my life that were trivial compared to world hunger but were seemingly huge to me in my world. From then on, I knew I could always run to God for protection when I was forced to flee from the hurtful and cruel words of others.

5. Do you need a safe place to run to today? If so, explain how running to God can help change your circumstances and, more important, your view of them.

Let's take a look at how Hagar discovered the magnificent truth that God sees all that is going on in our lives and that He ultimately cares. Read the following passage, Genesis 16:7-12 (NLT):

> The angel of the LORD found Hagar beside a desert spring along the road to Shur. The angel said to her, "Hagar, Sarai's servant, where have you come from, and where are you going?"
>
> "I am running away from my mistress," she replied.
>
> Then the angel of the LORD said, "Return to your mistress and submit to her authority." The angel added, "I will give you more descendants than you can count." And the angel also said, "You are now pregnant and will give birth to a son. You are to name him Ishmael, for the LORD has heard about your misery. This son of yours will be a wild one—free

and untamed as a wild donkey! He will be against everyone, and everyone will be against him. Yes, he will live at odds with the rest of his brothers."

6. Look at the questions the angel of the Lord asked Hagar in the first paragraph. What was the significance of asking about both her past and her future?

The Bible doesn't specifically tell us what abuse Hagar had to endure from Sarai. Since we know that she was a slave, it is safe to assume she had to endure brutal physical beatings and nasty verbal assaults. Sarai's jealousy and insecurity more than likely made her a cruel mistress. For Hagar, going back meant enduring more pain. It was more likely that she would be punished severely for running away. Perhaps you come from a background where abuse has been normal for you. For you it may have been physical. But as we discussed earlier, the abuse many of us are forced to endure comes in the form of a verbal attack that leaves us feeling worthless, unloved, and disrespected.

When we are coming out of a situation like that, it is important that we recognize where we are coming from so we can acknowledge our broken state. If we never admit that we are hurt by something, we cannot heal from it. The question "Where have you come from?" is significant because it forces us to admit that we are coming from a place where we have been wounded and broken. We cannot shrug it off as if it's no big deal, and we cannot lie and pretend that running was our choice when really it was our only means for survival.

If you have ever been abused either physically or verbally, it is important that you tell someone who can help you. In college I briefly dated a guy who verbally abused me, and I sunk into a brief period of depression after we broke up. My image of myself was tainted beyond belief. It wasn't until I finally opened up and told someone, "I was in a verbally abusive relationship," that I found healing. There is freedom and safety to be found in confiding in someone you trust.

There is also great significance in being asked where we are going. Many times we, like Hagar, flee a painful situation without a clearly outlined destination in mind. We just want out of our misery and away from the people causing it. If we are not careful, history will repeat itself in our lives and we will run directly into similar circumstances that will ultimately lead us to more pain and heartache. Growing up I traveled from group of friends to group of friends. Every time someone hurt me, I took off looking for a new group to hang with. Without fail, my new group would always hurt me as well. When we choose to examine what we are running from and where we are running to, we have a much better chance of finding a solution that will alleviate our pain and bring about the results we desire.

7. Examine your own life. Is there a hurt you have experienced that you haven't yet admitted to? If so, what is it? (For example, did a friend or sibling make a cutting remark that hurt your feelings and changed your relationship with him or her? Have you admitted that the hurt feelings that resulted from that stinging comment are what ultimately changed your relationship with that person? Or are you passing it off like you just grew apart?)

8. How can admitting that hurt help bring resolution to the way you have been feeling and your desire to run?

9. Think about a situation or person in your life that you are running from. Where are you running to and what do you hope to accomplish by running?

GOING BACK WITHOUT GOING BACKWARD

In Genesis 16:7-12, we discovered that Hagar was instructed to return to her mistress. Next week we will see that the end result was that Hagar was sent away some years later. I find it interesting that God sent Hagar back to her place of hurt even though it wasn't going to result in a peaceful and painless resolution and a restored relationship between Hagar and Sarai *and* Hagar and Abram.

10. Why do you think God sent Hagar back to face Sarai?

11. Is there someone in your life whom you need to go back and face? If so, who is it and what can be accomplished by your returning?

Notice, though, that God didn't send Hagar back to a sentence of misery. Instead, He promised her a blessing: "I will give you more descendants than you can count." Sarai's promise that she would be the mother of many nations was yet to come, as was the birth of Isaac. Yet God chose to speak a promise to Hagar first. He sent her back to the one who had hurt her with a fresh perspective on her own worth in the eyes of God. In essence, He was saying, "When you go back to Abram and Sarai, you will watch as I lavish blessings upon Sarai. But do not forget that I have lavished riches and blessings upon you as well. Sarai will be the mother of kings, but you will be the mother of princes." God did not send Hagar back to endure more abuse from Sarai. He didn't give her a life sentence of being worthless or unloved.

Instead, He spoke a great promise over her life regarding her future, and then He sent her back to make peace with her past.

12. Why do you think Hagar had to make peace with her past before embracing the future God had for her?

13. How can embracing a painful time in your own past help you embrace the future God has for you?

When I was four years old, my dad walked out on my mom and me. The year that followed was one of confusion and sorrow for me. I was too young to understand all of the things that had gone wrong in my parents' marriage. All I knew was that Daddy was gone and I visited him on weekends. The following year, my dad returned to my mom and sought restitution for the things he had done wrong. Now, thirty years after the day they first said, "I do," they are happily married.

But nineteen years passed between the time my dad returned to our family and the time when I forgave him for leaving. Over time I built up a resentment that never surfaced until I was ready to get married. And I had to go to my dad and talk about what had happened in the past so that I was fully able to embrace all God had for me in my future. At first I thought my own healing was where that story would end. But as I have shared my experience with girls and women across the world through writing and speaking, I have watched what God did in my life bring hope and healing to countless others. Facing my past brought me healing, it gave me strength and freedom to face my future, and it gave me the opportunity to minister to countless others who have experienced similar situations. There are, or will be, circumstances in your life that will present those same opportunities to you. Sometimes returning to face your past is the only option if you want to walk forward in healing.

A GOD-SIZED VIEW OF ALL THINGS

In Hagar's hour of deepest agony and loneliness, her view of God was ultimately changed. All of a sudden her eyes were opened to a God-sized view of all things. God was no longer some distant figure up in the sky but rather a real living, breathing God who took a great interest in her life. Read the following passage, Genesis 16:13-16 (NLT), before we begin to wrap up this week's lesson:

> Thereafter, Hagar referred to the LORD, who had spoken to her, as "the God who sees me," for she said, "I have seen the One who sees me!" Later that well was named Beer-lahairoi, and it can still be found between Kadesh and Bered.
> So Hagar gave Abram a son, and Abram named him Ishmael. Abram was eighty-six years old at that time.

Here we read that Hagar began referring to God as "the God who sees me," and we read that her son was named Ishmael, which means "God hears." Later in Hagar's story we will read about a time when she seems to lose hope, so it is important to note that this profound encounter with God didn't mean she never had doubts again. There will be times in all of our lives when we will have doubts or questions about the way God chooses to do things. The shift that occurred in Hagar's life here is not necessarily a shift in faith; instead it is a shift in relationship. God went from being *the* God to being *her* God, and that made all the difference in the world.

14. Think about your own faith for a moment. Is it simply a faith you "inherited" from your parents, or is it a faith that is truly your own? How do you know?

15. When you evaluate your own circumstances, what evidence is there that God sees, and God hears, what is going on in your life?

16. In her encounter with the angel of the Lord, Hagar's circum-
    stances weren't changed. In fact, she was sent back to the place
    she was running from. What was it about this encounter that
    changed her perspective of God (and of her circumstances) for
    the better? Explain.

17. Look back through the notes you have made during this week's
    lesson. Even if your circumstances have not changed, how has
    your perspective of God (and of your situation) changed, if it has
    changed at all? If it hasn't changed, why do you think that is?

18. Throughout Scripture, God's people give Him many names. Hagar wasn't the only one to personalize what she called Him. Look up the following three verses containing names of God and write each name (in Hebrew and English if your Bible gives you both) in the appropriate place.

    a. Genesis 22:14:

    b. Matthew 7:11:

    c. Psalm 23:1:

Giving God a personal name that is shared just between the two of you can be a great way to create deeper intimacy in your walk with the Lord. We should never treat the Lord, or His name, with any disrespect, but we can give Him a name of affection. A good friend of mine grew up without ever knowing her father. That left an enormous hole in her life that she had to learn to let God fill. In her personal prayers to the Lord, she began to refer to Him as "Abba," which is Hebrew for "Daddy." She did this to signify that she was allowing God to fill the void that an earthly father had left.

19. If you had to give God a personal name based on the role you see Him playing in your life, what would it be and why?

Ultimately, Hagar's story demonstrates that we can run from our circumstances but we cannot hide from God. In His love, He chases us and saves us from many of the poor choices we would make if we were left to ourselves. God desires that we become young women who are both whole and holy. Being whole requires us to face some of the things that hurt us so that we can forgive and be forgiven when it is necessary. Being holy requires us to strive to be like Christ to everyone we encounter, no matter how undeserving they may seem.

A few weeks ago we caught a glimpse into the personality of Sarai, and I can honestly say that she doesn't sound like the type of person I would want to go back and face and make things right with. Obedience that was directly linked to a great amount of love for an even greater God was the only thing that could have caused Hagar to retrace her steps. And often, it is the only thing that can get us to retrace our steps as well. Remember that this week, as you may have your own Sarai to return to.

Writing It Down

Before we end this week's lesson, write out a prayer to God, asking for forgiveness where you may need it and the strength to forgive those who have hurt you. Ask for wisdom in how to approach situations that may require you to trace a few of your steps.

Writing It Down

Now take a few moments to record a few key insights from this week.
What concepts or thoughts were new to you? Which ones were old
but seemed new because they were seen in fresh light? What impacted
you the most in this week's lesson? Why?

Setting a Higher Standard

Think of one personal goal you want to set for yourself as a result of this week's lesson. Write that goal out in detail, along with a brief description of how you will accomplish it. (For example, "I am going to talk with my dad about how his leaving our family has affected me over the years. I will start by finding a time when he and I can be alone and undistracted when we talk. Then I will write out what I want to say to him so I don't get nervous and forget. And I will make sure not to accuse him in our conversation, but I will share how I feel about things instead.") Write a date next to it so you can come back and check your progress.

week five

WHEN OLD SINS RESURFACE

As time went by and Isaac grew and was weaned,
Abraham gave a big party to celebrate the happy
occasion. But Sarah saw Ishmael—the son of Abraham
and her Egyptian servant Hagar—making fun of Isaac.
So she turned to Abraham and demanded, "Get rid of
that servant and her son. He is not going to share the
family inheritance with my son, Isaac. I won't have it!"

—GENESIS 21:8-10 (NLT)

A FEW WEEKS AGO, WE discussed what it's like to have a
ruthless person jealous of us and we examined Sarai's manipula-
tive behavior toward Hagar. We then saw Sarai's jealousy turn to
hatred and watched Hagar flee. Last week's lesson left off with Hagar
returning to Sarai, having a renewed relationship with God. This
week's lesson picks up several chapters, and many years, later. So
please review the following timeline to catch yourself up on all of
the material we are skipping. We are only briefly glancing at these
portions of Scripture because they pertain to the lives of Abram and
Sarai rather than to Hagar, the focal point of our study.

OVERVIEW OF TIMELINE BETWEEN GENESIS 16 AND GENESIS 21:

Genesis 17: God makes His covenant with Abram, changing his name to Abraham and promising to make him the "father of many nations." Sarai is renamed Sarah, and God promises to give Abraham a son through her.

Genesis 18: Three angels come to visit Abraham and prophesy that Sarah will have a son exactly one year after their visit. Sarah overhears from her tent and laughs. God asks Sarah why she laughs, and she denies laughing.

Genesis 19: Abraham's nephew Lot and Lot's daughters are spared, but the rest of Sodom and Gomorrah are destroyed.

Genesis 20: Abraham lies to Abimelech (a king) and tells him Sarah is his sister. Abimelech brings Sarah into his palace. God reveals to him that Sarah is married, and Abimelech gives Abraham land and sends him away (this closely resembles Abraham's previous encounter with Pharaoh in Egypt).

Now that you are caught up on the lives of Abraham and Sarah, let's pick up their story in Genesis 21 and begin this week's lesson. Once again, we will break our passage into smaller portions so we can digest each section as we go.

Then the LORD did exactly what he had promised. Sarah became pregnant, and she gave a son to Abraham in his old age. It all happened at the time God had said it would. And Abraham named his son Isaac. Eight days after Isaac was born, Abraham circumcised him as God had commanded. Abraham was one hundred years old at the time. (Genesis 21:1-5, NLT)

FILL IN THE BLANKS

1. What did God do for Abraham and Sarah?

The LORD _____ and did for Sarah _____

_____.

2. What happened to Sarah?

She _____, and she _____ to

_____ in his _____.

3. When did it happen?

It all happened _____ God had _____

_____.

This is significant information because it sets us up for the point of this week's lesson. Here we see that God performed a miracle for Sarah (as she was well past the age of childbearing) and fulfilled His promise to Abraham. You would think such a happy occasion would delight Sarah and would erase any pain or jealousy she had over not being able to bear a son earlier. But we will soon see that even a happy occasion cannot permanently hide roots of bitterness or jealousy we have refused to deal with. Let's read on together:

> And Sarah declared, "God has brought me laughter! All who hear about this will laugh with me. For who would have dreamed that I would ever have a baby? Yet I have given Abraham a son in his old age!" (Genesis 21:6-7, NLT)

4. God brought Sarah laughter. What emotion does laughter convey?

As time went by and Isaac grew and was weaned, Abraham gave a big party to celebrate the happy occasion. But Sarah saw Ishmael—the son of Abraham and her Egyptian servant Hagar—making fun of Isaac. So she turned to Abraham and demanded, "Get rid of that servant and her son. He is not going to share the family inheritance with my son, Isaac. I won't have it!" (Genesis 21:8-10, NLT)

5. What do you think Sarah felt when she saw Ishmael making fun of Isaac?

LAUGHTER TURNS TO JEALOUSY

Sarah's easygoing laughter quickly turned into angry demands. It is especially important to note that she didn't refer to Hagar by her name here. She was "that servant." When Sarah saw something that threatened her, she began hurling insults. And she seemed to conveniently forget that Ishmael was also Abraham's son—his firstborn son—and that an inheritance was his birthright. It also seemed to slip Sarah's mind entirely that Ishmael was brought into existence only because of demands Sarah made years ago. It was as if looking at Ishmael was a glaring reminder of a time in her life when she lacked faith, and it was constant proof that Hagar the slave woman was Sarah's equal when it came to giving Abraham an heir.

In previous weeks, we learned that both Sarah and Hagar had jealousy problems. Sarah was jealous of Hagar's ability to conceive, and Hagar was jealous of Sarah's position. It's safe to assume that both women dealt with their jealousy issues over time. A few weeks ago, we learned that God sent Hagar back to face Sarah and deal with the issues she had with her. This week we see that Sarah was able to conceive her own miracle baby and had her own son. She no longer had any need to be jealous of Hagar—yet she was. And when she saw Ishmael (who was probably a teenager by now) snickering at Isaac, Sarah decided to abuse her position and cast both Hagar and Ishmael out. Hagar may have been enslaved to Sarah, but it is obvious that Sarah was still enslaved to her insecurities.

6. What are some things you feel insecure about? What circumstances trigger feelings of insecurity for you?

7. Why do you think things still tend to resurface long after we let them go?

8. Do you think we are ever completely free of our insecurities? Why or why not?

WORDS TO MEMORIZE

It's time to get out your 3x5 cards again. This week's verse is one I am sure you have heard countless times, but it should never grow old in our hearts. Commit this verse to memory this week and you will always have it handy for the many times you will need it.

> So here's what I want you to do, God helping you: Take your everyday, ordinary life—your sleeping, eating, going-to-work, and walking-around life—and place it before God as an offering. Embracing what God does for you is the best thing you can do for him. Don't become so well-adjusted to your culture that you fit into it without even thinking. Instead, fix your attention on God. You'll be changed from the inside out. Readily recognize what he wants from you, and quickly respond to it. Unlike the culture around you, always dragging you down to its level of immaturity, God brings the best out of you, develops well-formed maturity in you. (Romans 12:1-2)

This verse talks about being changed from the inside out. It also tells us that the culture around us will constantly drag us down to its level of immaturity while God will work hard to bring out the best in us. Another way to put it is, the world will bring out the worst in us so God can get rid of it and put His best in us. When areas of insecurity or sin resurface in our lives, it is usually because God wants to help us get rid of them for good. If we are to ever get rid of something once and for all, we have to make sure there are no hidden traces of it remaining somewhere in our system. I have seen God do this many times in my own life.

IS SHE OVER IT?

Because we are all dealing with our own unique circumstances, it can be tough to find a quiz that will give us accurate results about ourselves. But sometimes it's easier for us to recognize undercover sin in the lives of others than it is for us to see it in ourselves. So take the following quiz and see if the girl described in the scenario below is really over what happened to her. Then take what you see in her and examine your own heart to learn if there is any unforgiveness, anger, or bitterness lurking in you.

Scenario: Katie attends a large high school with a bunch of people she has gone to school with since kindergarten. She has had a crush on Nick since the seventh grade. In her junior year he asks her to the prom, but she can't go because her parents won't let her go to the prom until she is a senior. So Nick asks Katie's best friend, Susan, who gladly accepts the invitation. Susan knows that Katie has been in love with Nick for years, but she goes to prom with him anyway and even lets him kiss her good night. After a monthlong fight with Susan, Katie forgives her and says that things are fine between them. You be the judge of how truthful she is being. After reading each statement below, determine whether or not Katie is hiding her true feelings. Circle "O" for over it or "L" for lying about it.

1. Susan has a photo of Nick and her at prom taped to the front of her binder with a bunch of photos from other events. When she sees it, Katie puts a book on top of Susan's binder so she doesn't have to look at it.

   O   L

2. Katie's mom tells her that she was surprised to hear that Tom, the youth pastor, chaperoned the prom. Katie uses the opportunity to say, "See, you should have let me go."

   O   L

3. All of her friends are talking about the hideous dress that another girl was wearing. Katie quickly gets up and goes to the restroom so she doesn't have to feel left out.

   O   L

4. Katie sees Nick staring at Susan across the room and fights the urge to cry.

   O   L

5. When Nick comes up and sits next to Katie at lunch and asks how she's doing, she quickly mumbles something and leaves.

   O   L

Correct Answers: "L" for all five questions. Hurt feelings can emerge in tons of different ways, and this quiz showed only five examples of how Katie could have been hiding her true feelings. We saw her react in disgust when she saw Susan's binder, she treated her mom with disrespect when the topic of prom came up, she was uncomfortable around her friends when she couldn't relate, her heart was still broken over not being able to go to prom with Nick, and she reacted in anger when Nick asked how she was.

9. Did Katie's story give you insights into any emotions you might be hiding that could turn into sin if you don't deal with them? If so, what are they and how can you deal with them?

DIFFERENT DESERT, DIFFERENT ATTITUDE

This week's lesson finds Hagar in the desert once again. But this desert is different from the one she first ran to for escape, and we will see that her demeanor is much different this time as well. Let's resume our story with Genesis 21:11-16 (NLT):

> [Sending Ishmael and Hagar away] upset Abraham very much because Ishmael was his son. But God told Abraham, "Do not be upset over the boy and your servant wife. Do just as Sarah says, for Isaac is the son through whom your descendants will be counted. But I will make a nation of the descendants of Hagar's son because he also is your son."
>
> So Abraham got up early the next morning, prepared food for the journey, and strapped a container of water to Hagar's shoulders. He sent her away with their son, and she walked out into the wilderness of Beersheba, wandering aimlessly. When the water was gone, she left the boy in the shade of a bush. Then she went and sat down by herself about a hundred yards away. "I don't want to watch the boy die," she said, as she burst into tears.

So many thoughts come to my mind as I read this passage. Hagar must have felt an entire gamut of emotions as Abraham sent her away from her home with their son. The feeling of being used by Abraham and Sarah just to get a son probably resurfaced as she realized there was no place for her or Ishmael in Abraham's family now that Sarah—his *real* wife—had given him Isaac. She more than likely felt rejected by Sarah, whom she had tried to make peace with over the years.

Perhaps she even thought things were going well between them up until this moment. And I am sure Hagar was filled with terror as she realized that she had absolutely nowhere to go and this time couldn't go back. Because she was in the middle of such a horrible situation, she must have felt as if God had forgotten her. In moments when we feel as if God has forgotten us, even running into His arms doesn't feel safe.

10. Out of all the feelings mentioned in the previous two paragraphs (used, rejected, surprised, afraid, forgotten), which one do you think you would have felt the deepest if you were Hagar? Why?

11. Which feeling can you relate to most in your own life? Explain.

12. Has there ever been a time in your life when you felt as if God had not been faithful to you? If so, what happened and how did you work through it?

Let's go back to Hagar's previous desert experience with God for a moment so we can compare the two situations. Please read the following passage, Genesis 16:7-14 (NLT):

The angel of the LORD found Hagar beside a desert spring along the road to Shur. The angel said to her, "Hagar, Sarai's servant, where have you come from, and where are you going?"

"I am running away from my mistress," she replied.

Then the angel of the LORD said, "Return to your mistress and submit to her authority." The angel added, "I will give you more descendants than you can count." And the angel also said, "You are now pregnant and will give birth to a son. You are to name him Ishmael, for the LORD has heard about your misery. This son of yours will be a wild one—free and untamed as a wild donkey! He will be against everyone, and everyone will be against him. Yes, he will live at odds with the rest of his brothers."

Thereafter, Hagar referred to the LORD, who had spoken to her, as "the God who sees me," for she said, "I have seen the

One who sees me!" Later that well was named Beer-lahairoi, and it can still be found between Kadesh and Bered.

13. What did Hagar call God during her first desert experience?

   "_____ me."

14. Fourteen years have passed, and now Hagar is back in the desert, sobbing and saying, "I don't want to watch the boy die." Do you think she's still calling God "the God who sees me"? What makes you say that?

15. Have you ever forgotten who God is during a time when tragedy has found you? If so, explain.

16. How did you get back to a place of renewed faith?

One of the most astounding things in all of this is that Hagar's second trip to the desert wasn't the result of anything that was directly her fault. Sarah flew into a jealous rage when she saw *Ishmael* making fun of Isaac. The Bible doesn't tell us that Hagar was even there.

17. In Genesis 16:12, the Bible gives us insight into Ishmael's personality and disposition. Read the verse (back on page 91) and then describe Ishmael in the following space.

18. Do you think Hagar had any chance at controlling a son like that?

19. Have you ever been punished for something someone else did? If so, explain what happened and how you felt. (Examples: Your parents got divorced, and now you hardly ever get to see one of your parents and maybe even some of your siblings. Or your brother broke your mom's favorite lamp, and you both got grounded for it.)

20. Have you ever experienced a decline in your own faith? If so, what caused it?

21. Why is it easy to lose heart so quickly?

And we know that God causes everything to work together for the good of those who love God and are called according to his purpose for them. (Romans 8:28, NLT)

In moments when it is hard for us to understand why everything seems to be going wrong, we need to remember that God is constantly at work putting together something good for us that will ultimately lead to His glory. Things that work together for our good are not always good things. Last year my grandfather, whom I was very close to, fell ill quickly and went into the hospital and passed away. Losing him was not the answer anyone in my family wanted. We were absolutely grief-stricken and stunned by the whole thing.

But a few months after his passing, my grandma sold her house and moved in with my parents. For the first time in her old age, she had someone to take care of her. During the last several years of my grandpa's life, she had to care for him in ways that were taxing on her. Although she missed him greatly, she was able to experience a much less laborious schedule. She knew that keeping him here with us would have only prolonged his suffering. When he passed away, we knew that he had gone on to be with Jesus, and that brought my grandma the joy and freedom she needed to enjoy her later years. In the past several months, she has thrived and come to life in ways I haven't seen in years. Losing my grandpa wasn't good, but it worked for good in the life of my grandma.

22. Has there been a time in your own life when you have watched God make circumstances that weren't good into something good? If so, what was it and how did you feel at the time?

23. Is there a circumstance in your life right now that isn't good that you would like to see God work together for good? If so, take a moment and write out a prayer asking Him to come through for you in this circumstance. He will most certainly answer you, even if it's not in the way you would most desire.

Talking It Out

As you wrap up this week's lesson, write out a prayer to God asking Him to help you uncover some of the hidden emotions and sins in your own life so you can deal with them once and for all.

Writing It Down

Take a few moments and journal any thoughts you have about this week's lesson. Was there any new truth that really stuck out to you? If so, what was it?

Setting a Higher Standard

Set one new goal for yourself as a result of this week's lesson. My goal is to take one hour sometime during this next week and spend time alone with God really examining my heart and asking Him to reveal problem areas to me. If you decide to use this as your goal, make sure the alone time with God is really alone time—no cell phone, no Internet, no distractions whatsoever. Just you and God and an honest evaluation of your heart!

week six

WHERE SHE LEFT HIM

Then God heard the boy's cries, and the angel of
God called to Hagar from the sky, "Hagar, what's
wrong? Do not be afraid! God has heard the boy's
cries from the place where you laid him. Go to him
and comfort him, for I will make a great nation from
his descendants."

—GENESIS 21:17-18 (NLT)

DURING THE LAST FIVE WEEKS, we have traveled through
some pretty emotional times with Hagar. We were with her when she
was used by others for their own gain, we traveled with her through
her rocky relationship with Sarai, and we accompanied her on two
different adventures into the wilderness. In fact, last week we left her
crying her eyes out in the desert. But it wouldn't be fair to leave her
there. So before we leave her for the last time, let's pick up the story
and discover the hope that she finds. We'll read all of Genesis 21:1-21
to recap for context:

> GOD visited Sarah exactly as he said he would; GOD did to
> Sarah what he promised: Sarah became pregnant and gave
> Abraham a son in his old age, and at the very time God
> had set. Abraham named him Isaac. When his son was

eight days old, Abraham circumcised him just as God had commanded.

Abraham was a hundred years old when his son Isaac was born.

Sarah said,

> God has blessed me with laughter
> and all who get the news will laugh with me!

She also said,

> Whoever would have suggested to Abraham
> that Sarah would one day nurse a baby!
> Yet here I am! I've given the old man a son!

The baby grew and was weaned. Abraham threw a big party on the day Isaac was weaned.

One day Sarah saw the son that Hagar the Egyptian had borne to Abraham, poking fun at her son Isaac. She told Abraham, "Get rid of this slave woman and her son. No child of this slave is going to share inheritance with my son Isaac!"

The matter gave great pain to Abraham—after all, Ishmael was his son. But God spoke to Abraham, "Don't feel badly about the boy and your maid. Do whatever Sarah tells you. Your descendants will come through Isaac. Regarding your maid's son, be assured that I'll also develop a great nation from him—he's your son, too."

Abraham got up early the next morning, got some food together and a canteen of water for Hagar, put them on her back and sent her away with the child. She wandered off into the desert of Beersheba. When the water was gone, she left the child under a shrub and went off, fifty yards or so. She said, "I can't watch my son die." As she sat, she broke into sobs.

Meanwhile, God heard the boy crying. The angel of God called from Heaven to Hagar, "What's wrong, Hagar? Don't be afraid. God has heard the boy and knows the fix he's in. Up now; go get the boy. Hold him tight. I'm going to make of him a great nation."

Just then God opened her eyes. She looked. She saw a well of water. She went to it and filled her canteen and gave the boy a long, cool drink.

God was on the boy's side as he grew up. He lived out in the desert and became a skilled archer. He lived in the Paran wilderness. And his mother got him a wife from Egypt.

WE CAN FIND HIM WHERE WE LEFT HIM

1. What did God do? Please fill in the blanks.

   "Meanwhile, God _____ the _____."

2. Look back at Genesis 16:13 on page 91. In that verse, what did Hagar say that God does?

God has proven to be the God who sees and the God who hears over and over again in Hagar's life, and I am sure He has done the same in your life too. Even when Hagar had forgotten about God hearing and seeing her needs, He came through for her. When Hagar thought her promise from God would surely go unfulfilled, God reminded her of it. He gave Hagar and Ishmael a well in the desert to revive their bodies, and He sent a word of encouragement to revive their souls. Oh what a compassionate God we serve!

Read the following verse, Genesis 16:7 (NLT):

The angel of the LORD found Hagar beside a desert spring along the road to Shur.

3. Where did the angel of the Lord find Hagar during her first desert encounter?

    "The angel of the LORD found Hagar _____

    _____, along the road to Shur."

Read the following verse, Genesis 21:19 (NLT):

Then God opened Hagar's eyes, and she saw a well. She immediately filled her water container and gave the boy a drink.

4. Where was Hagar when God opened her eyes?

    "God opened Hagar's eyes, and she saw _____."

Now, bear with me a minute as I make the connection between these two verses for us. Dictionary.com tells us that a well is "a spring or natural source of water." And in Jamieson, Fausset, and Brown's *Bible Commentary*, they state that Hagar intended to head out in the same direction she did in Genesis 16, although she may have gotten a little lost.[3] So even though she wasn't in the exact same spot, Hagar was wandering around in the same desert. And she stumbled across a spring in the ground that she couldn't see until God pointed it out to her.

I don't think it is ironic that she left God at a spring in Genesis 16 and later found Him at another spring in Genesis 21. Sometimes when distance builds in our relationship with God, it is because we have left Him—not because He has left us. When this happens, we can usually find God right where we left Him.

5. Has there ever been a time in your life when you have felt far from God? If so, can you trace your steps back to a time when you left God and His ways for your own? If so, explain.

6. If you have ever wandered away from God temporarily, how did you find your way back to Him?

A PERSONAL GOD WITH PERSONAL TOUCHES

Sometimes when we have left God, we don't have to retrace all of our steps back to Him—we can simply find our way by calling out to Him. That's what happened in Hagar's case. She wasn't in the exact spot she had left God, but she was close. She cried out, and He came to her rescue.

God has come to my rescue many times before. But one time still stands tallest in my memory. When I was fifteen years old, I had to have major surgery. I was absolutely terrified and uncertain about what my future would hold. A few days before my surgery, I was reading about Noah in my daily quiet time and it fascinated me that God gave him a rainbow as a sign of His promise to never flood the earth again.

Lord, where's my rainbow? I silently prayed as I begged God for a sign that everything would be okay. Silence greeted me. And with fear in my heart, I went into the operating room. A few hours later, after a much longer and more extensive surgery than the doctors had initially anticipated, I was wheeled from the recovery room to my own hospital room. My mom was with me, but my dad was nowhere to be found. A few moments later, he came flying into my room and threw back the curtains.

"You've got to see this," he said to me. Groggy from medication, I shielded my eyes from the light.

"Shannon, look," he said. And when I did, the most magnificent rainbow I had ever seen met my eyes. A few moments later a nurse came in.

"Did you guys see that rainbow?" she asked. "I have never seen anything like that before." And I smiled to myself, knowing that God had sent that rainbow just for me. Even now as I write this, my eyes tear up at the thought of that story. The fact that God would care that much about calming my fears amazes me. I'm sure many people can rationalize away my miracle, but I won't listen. I wholeheartedly believe in the God who put a well in the desert for Hagar and a rainbow in the sky for me. But please don't think that means I never have doubts about my current circumstances.

Just like Hagar, I still find myself crying in the desert, afraid that God will fail me and my life will fall apart. But He doesn't. Time and time again He has come through for me, even if it's not always in the way I expected or preferred. As I write this, ten years have passed since God put a rainbow in the sky for me. And rainbows still serve as tangible reminders that God cares for me. On my honeymoon in Maui in 2005, I saw a rainbow from my hotel room window, and I smiled at the reminder that I was walking forward into the wonderful future God had put together for me. Rainbows have become sort of a shared smile between me and a God I can't physically see.

7. Do you have an experience that seems like a shared smile between you and God? If so, what is it? If not, write out a prayer asking God to show Himself to you in a unique and special way.

WORDS TO LIVE BY

For the last time during this study, it is time to get out your 3x5 cards so you can write down this week's memory verse. It is one I call to my mind frequently, and I am sure it will be for you, too.

> This is GOD's Message, the God who made earth, made it livable and lasting, known everywhere as GOD: "Call to me and I will answer you. I'll tell you marvelous and wondrous things that you could never figure out on your own." (Jeremiah 33:2-3)

8. Hagar wasn't the only person in Scripture who had God come through for her in a big way when she called to Him. Look up and read the following two passages. Next to each reference, write the name of the person God came through for and what the miracle was.

    a. Daniel 3:19-30:

b. 1 Samuel 17:32-51:

9. Describe how you think Hagar felt when she saw the well.

The Bible says, "Then God opened Hagar's eyes, and she saw a well" (Genesis 21:19, NLT), which leads me to believe that the well had been there all along. Sometimes the very answers to our desperate cries are right in front of us, if only we would notice them. This week make a conscious effort to start looking for the answers, and the blessings, that God has placed all around you but you have somehow become oblivious to.

10. How can you become more aware of the blessings and the answers to prayer that God has surrounded you with?

11. What are the top three things that tend to distract you from seeing God at work in your life? (For instance, a busy schedule, non-Christian friends, or obsession with a boy.)

12. How can you begin to weed those distractions out of your life and make more of an effort to put the focus on Christ?

ON YOUR SIDE

Before we close this week, I think it is important to note one more thing we read in this passage. Please look at Genesis 21:20-21 with me:

> God was on the boy's side as he grew up. He lived out in the desert and became a skilled archer. He lived in the Paran wilderness. And his mother got him a wife from Egypt.

13. In what ways do you think God was on Ishmael's side as he grew up?

Hagar and Ishmael were sent into the desert because Sarah flew into a jealous rage. Abraham—Ishmael's dad—took Sarah's side over Ishmael and Hagar's. The world was against them. Death looked imminent. But God came through for them because He was on their side. In your life you will experience times when it seems as if no one is on your side. Moments of loneliness are inevitable. But it is important to remember that even in those dark moments, God is on your side.

One of my favorite verses is Joshua 1:5-6. You can choose to memorize this verse this week if you prefer it over the other option (on page 107).

"In the same way I was with Moses, I'll be with you. I won't give up on you; I won't leave you. Strength! Courage!"

14. What significance does this verse have to you personally?

15. Think of a tough situation you have to face on a regular basis. How does knowing that God is on your side make things better? Explain.

WHEN THE CRITICS AREN'T CLAPPING

There are going to be people in our lives who will criticize us. You, too, will have your share of Sarahs who love you when they want to use you for something and then can't stand you when you have something they don't. And your life will also be sprinkled with several Abrahams: those who wish you well but don't have the courage to stand up for you when the moment arises. You will even have your Isaacs: the favored sons (or, in our case, daughters) whom you will never quite be able to live up to.

16. Think through your life for a moment. Identify the following people in your circumstances if you can.

    a. Sarah:

b. Abraham:

c. Isaac:

17. Write out a prayer asking God to bless each of those people you just listed, and ask Him for help in loving them.

The truth is, it doesn't matter how many Sarahs, Abrahams, or Isaacs we have in our lives. What matters is that we have God in our lives and on our sides. That's what made the difference in Hagar's life. It is my prayer that as we have spent these past few weeks traveling through Hagar's life together you have come to see God at work in unfavorable circumstances and in the life of an unlikely girl.

When we began our study together, I reminded you that Hagar wasn't a superstar. She always played more of a supporting role to Sarah in the spotlight. Yet God saw and heard the needs in Hagar's life, and His light shined brightly in her story. God sees and hears all of the happenings in your life, too. And it is His desire to shine brightly through you as well. Who really wants to be in the spotlight anyway when you can have God shine His bright light of love through you?

Hagar's circumstances never seemed to change for the better, and she was never promoted to the role of queen or princess. In fact, the last we ever hear of her is here in the desert by the spring where she found God for a second time. But there is really no better place we can leave her than in the loving hands of God. And as you and I part ways at the end of this study, I know there is no better place I can leave you than in the loving hands of God.

18. Why is it significant that Hagar's circumstances never seemed to change?

19. Just for fun, speculate about what you think happened to Hagar after she left the spring in the desert that day. For instance, the Bible says she found Ishmael a wife from Egypt. Do you think Hagar went back home? If so, do you think she returned to a life of slavery? Or was Sarah's anger a blessing in disguise that actually served to set Hagar free?

20. When you think of God shining His light through you, what are some practical ways you see that happening? Explain.

Talking It Out

Write out a prayer to the Lord thanking Him for all He taught you in this study and asking for strength and courage to apply it to your daily life.

Writing It Down

Take a few moments to reflect on Hagar's story. Write down a few points that really resonated deeply with you, and explain why you think you connected with those points so much.

Setting a Higher Standard

Write down one new goal you have for yourself as a result of this week's lesson or our study as a whole. Make sure to break your goal down into smaller steps, and don't forget to write a date next to it so you can come back and check your progress.

note to leaders

HOW TO USE THIS BIBLE STUDY IN A SMALL GROUP

WHETHER YOU ARE A VETERAN small-group leader or a rookie taking the field for the first time, it's important that you outline for your group what is expected of them. To help you think through how you want to do things, I offer you six steps I always take when facilitating a small group. You know your group of girls best, so pick and choose from my suggestions what will work for them. But more than anything else, have fun as you lead them through God's Word—and Hagar's story—together.

1. At your very first session together, it is important that you go over the rules of confidentiality that you want your group to adhere to. During the course of your time together, some girls in the group may open up about struggles they are facing or painful experiences from their past. It is your job as the group leader to make sure your girls know that things shared with

the group must stay within the group and should not be discussed outside your regular meetings.

2. Since girls have a tendency to talk—a lot—and sometimes get off track, you will need to establish a set length of time for the discussion portion of your group meetings. Some groups may have only half an hour, while others may be able to devote an entire hour. No matter what you decide, be consistent. This will help keep girls engaged and on course. You can also use it as a tool when things get off topic by saying something like, "While this is all good stuff you are talking about, we have only thirty minutes to discuss this week's lesson. So let's save all of these other conversations until after the meeting is over."

3. In your group you will have a variety of personality types. Even if all of the girls are friends outside the group, you will still notice that some of them talk more than others. To keep the group balanced and in order to make everyone feel included, monitor how much one person shares and make note of those who don't seem to open up at all. Try to encourage everyone to talk at least once during group time.

4. I have found that opening each week with an icebreaker question or game puts everyone at ease and gets some of the nervous energy out before actual group discussion begins. Having girls share embarrassing moments, favorite ice cream flavors, or middle names can be a good way to get to know the girls in your group while getting everyone settled in.

5. On average, each week in this Bible study has close to thirty questions for the girls to answer on their own before you meet. Because you will not have time to go over all of their answers in your group time, it will be best for you to go through each lesson before you meet and select five to seven questions you would like your girls to discuss. The first five questions in each week's lesson aren't always the most thought-provoking, so look over all of the questions and see which ones your girls

need to give special thought to. Start your discussion with those.

6. Every time I lead a small group, I like to encourage the girls to be thinking about each other outside the group. This helps them strengthen their relationships with each other and build trust. I hand out 3x5 cards at the end of every group meeting and have the girls write their name and e-mail address or phone number on the top line, and several prayer requests on the lines below. Then I collect all of the cards and let the girls pick a card from a basket. They are responsible for praying for the person they picked and contacting her to encourage her sometime during the week. In all of the groups I have led, girls always list this as one of their favorite parts of the study. Feel free to use your own version of this.

Have a great time with your group!
Shannon

NOTES

1. Geoffrey W. Bromiley, *The International Standard Bible Encyclopedia*, Volume 1 (Grand Rapids, MI: Eerdmans, 1979), 593; Ann Spangler and Jean E. Syswerda, *Women of the Bible* (Grand Rapids, MI: Zondervan, 1999), 25, 32.

2. Ann Spangler and Jean E. Syswerda, *Women of the Bible* (Grand Rapids, MI: Zondervan, 1999), 25, 32.

3. Robert Jamieson, A. R. Fausset, and David Brown, *Bible Commentary*, Volume 1 Genesis–Esther (Peabody, MA: Hendrickson, 2002), 170.

ABOUT THE AUTHOR

TWENTYSOMETHING AUTHOR SHANNON PRIMICERIO resides in Southern California with her husband, Michael. The Primicerios are a fun-loving couple who enjoy watching baseball, playing bocce ball, flying kites, and hanging out at the beach.

Shannon has a BA in journalism and a minor in biblical studies from Biola University. She was the recipient of the *North County Times* "Excellence in Writing" award in 2000 and the San Diego Christian Writers Guild "Nancy Bayless Award for Excellence in Writing" in 2003.

She has been interviewed on radio and television programs across the nation and was recently featured in such media outlets as PBS's *Religion and Ethics Newsweekly*, *The Harvest Show*, and *TIME* magazine.

Shannon's ministry spans the globe, as her books are available in several languages. Her books include *The Divine Dance*, *God Called a Girl*, the BEING A GIRL . . . series, and *Life. Now.* (the last of which she cowrote with Michael).

She also serves as a mentor to young authors through the Jerry B. Jenkins Christian Writers Guild. Her articles have appeared in *Marriage Partnership* and *BRIO* magazines.

To learn more about Shannon, please visit www.beingagirlbooks .com. You can also contact her via e-mail at shannon@ beingagirlbooks.com.

TWO MORE EXCITING STUDIES FOR TEEN GIRLS!

Author Shannon Primicerio takes a fresh approach to devotional studies by leading you through the lives of three very different women of the Bible: Hagar, Leah, and Miriam. Throughout the TRUELIFE BIBLE STUDIES series, you'll explore each woman's relationship with God, connect with core issues, and discover relevant lessons that can apply to your lives today.

Leah
ISBN-13: 978-1-60006-112-7
ISBN-10: 1-60007-112-5

Leah's story offers us valuable lessons in popularity, jealousy, unhealthy competition, and the search for true love.

Miriam
SBN-13: 978-1-60006-114-1
ISBN-10: 1-60006-114-1

Although she was often overshadowed by her more famous brothers, Moses and Aaron, courageous leader Miriam played a vital role in the Hebrews' delivery from Egypt.

THINK

NAVPRESS
BRINGING TRUTH TO LIFE
www.navpress.com

To order copies, visit your local Christian bookstore, call NavPress at 1-800-366-7788, or log on to www.navpress.com.
To locate a Christian bookstore near you, call 1-800-991-7747.